HAVE A Positive IMPACT...

...ON THE Planet

by Charis Mather

KidHaven PUBLISHING

Published in 2025 by
KidHaven Publishing, an Imprint of
Greenhaven Publishing, LLC
2544 Clinton St., Buffalo, NY 14224

Written by: Charis Mather
Edited by: Robin Twiddy
Designed by: Danielle Rippengill

All facts, statistics, web addresses and URLs in this book were verified as valid and accurate at time of writing. No responsibility for any changes to external websites or references can be accepted by either the author or publisher.

Cataloging-in-Publication Data

Names: Mather, Charis, 1999-.
Title: On the planet / Charis Mather.
Description: Buffalo, New York : KidHaven Publishing, 2025. | Series: Have a positive impact... | Includes glossary and index.
Identifiers: ISBN 9781534547490 (pbk.) | ISBN 9781534547506 (library bound) | ISBN 9781534547513 (ebook)
Subjects: LCSH: Environmentalism--Juvenile literature. | Children and the environment--Juvenile literature. | Social action--Juvenile literature.
Classification: LCC GE195.5 M38 2025 | DDC 333.72--dc23

Manufactured in the United States of America

CPSIA compliance information: Batch #CSKH25
For further information contact Greenhaven Publishing LLC at 1-844-317-7404.

Please visit our website, www.greenhavenpublishing.com.
For a free color catalog of all our high-quality books, call toll free 1-844-317-7404 or fax 1-844-317-7405.

Find us on

Contents

Words that look like this are explained in the glossary on page 31.

You AND THE World

All over the world, people like you are changing our planet. The world is huge, but every single person on it makes a difference. Did you know that the things you do can change things all the way on the other side of the world? It sounds unbelievable, but it's true!

Making an Impact

When we do things that affect the world, we can say we have had an impact. Changing the world for the better starts with learning about the impact that our lives have on the environment.

People impact the world in many different ways. Riding a bicycle instead of taking the car somewhere can have a positive impact on the world. Even something as simple as following a path instead of going through a field makes a difference!

Staying on a path protects the plants and animals nearby.

Positive impacts on the environment make the world a healthier place. Everything we do, from what we eat to what we wear, changes the world bit by bit.

Out of Sight, Out of Mind?

At first, it may be hard to see the impact that we have on the environment. Think about the garbage we throw away at home. Where does it go? Just because we cannot see it anymore does not mean that the garbage does not have an impact on the planet.

SOME GARBAGE, SUCH AS GLASS, PAPER, METAL, AND SOME PLASTICS, CAN BE RECYCLED AND USED AGAIN.

A lot of the trash that comes from our homes goes into landfill sites or is burned. Over time, landfill pollution goes into our air, water, and land.

Part of the Ecosystem

You might not see where your garbage goes, but the pollution from it affects the whole planet. We impact and are impacted by everything around us, just like in an ecosystem. Living and nonliving things in an ecosystem affect each other a lot!

Birds help bring seeds to new ground so that plants can grow.

Environmentally Minded

We are connected to the environment around us, so it is important to think about our impact on it. This is called being environmentally minded. Being environmentally minded helps us make choices that have a positive effect on the world around us.

Informed Decisions

If we want to keep our environment healthy, we should make informed decisions about how to help it. An informed decision is a choice that is based on information. The more information we have, the easier it is to make positive choices.

We make informed decisions all the time, even when we get dressed. If you see rain outside your window, you can make an informed decision to wear a raincoat. If it is sunny, you might choose shorts.

Researching

If you were traveling somewhere new, how would you know what to wear? You could still make an informed decision by researching what the weather is like in different places. Researching is collecting information from different places, things, and people. We call these sources.

Doing research is a good way to make informed decisions about the environment. When we know which of our actions hurt the environment, we can make different choices.

Reusing the same cloth shopping bag is better than using new plastic bags every time.

Researching Right

There is so much that we can learn about our planet. There are many good sources we can use to research the environment. Let's look at a few ...

BOOKS

Books are a great way to research. Nonfiction books are filled with facts about the world and often have real pictures. The book you are reading right now is a nonfiction book. You're already on your way to researching right!

CHECK OUT THE NONFICTION SECTION THE NEXT TIME YOU'RE AT A LIBRARY.

Experts

Experts are people who know a lot about something. Environmental groups are usually full of experts on the environment.

Spending Time Outside

You can learn a lot by making your own observations. Spending time outside helps you to get in touch with nature and see how the plants and animals in an ecosystem are connected.

ALWAYS BE SAFE WHEN USING THE INTERNET. ASK AN ADULT TO HELP YOU FIND GOOD SOURCES.

The Internet

The Internet is often used to share new information. Lots of environmental experts put what they learn on the Internet. See if you can find a video online to help you learn about our planet.

Telling Fact from Fiction

While there are many sources that we can use to research the environment, we have to be careful to choose ones with true information. If a source gives true, up-to-date facts about something, it is called a reliable source.

YOU CAN'T MAKE AN INFORMED DECISION WITH OUT-OF-DATE OR FALSE INFORMATION.

Up to date

Having up-to-date information is important because old information might not be true anymore, even if it was before. Using out-of-date information is like trying to choose what to wear based on what the weather was like last week, instead of what it is like today. You might end up going out in the rain without a raincoat!

Sources that have information based on opinions are not good sources. An opinion is an idea about something that is not based on facts.

Reliable Sources on the Internet

It can be tricky to figure out which sources on the internet are good and which aren't. The last few letters of an internet address can help us find sources that we can trust. Look for these letters:

.gov
.org
.edu

FALSE INFORMATION SPREADS VERY QUICKLY, ESPECIALLY ON THE INTERNET.

Even when a source looks reliable, it is always good to check that another reliable source agrees with the information in it.

Activism

Learning about the problems in the world can make people feel strongly about making it a better place. When people want to make big changes, they sometimes take part in activism.

Activism is when people do or say something to bring attention to problems that they care a lot about. Activists hope that bringing attention will cause changes that help the world and the people in it.

Protesting

One way that activists get people to pay attention is by protesting where lots of people can see them. Protesting is when people who share the same beliefs meet together to try to make a change happen. They often have signs that they use to raise awareness.

Letter Writing

Another way to get attention for a serious problem is by sending letters to people who have the power to make big changes. Activists who are worried about the environment hope that their letters will change the rules we have about protecting the planet.

TRY WRITING YOUR OWN LETTER TO SOMEONE ABOUT A CHANGE YOU WOULD LIKE TO SEE.

Animal Rights

Many activists and environmentalists work to protect animals from the impact of people. They believe that animals should have rights to keep them safe. Rights are the ability to have or do things based on your own choices and needs.

Many animals are used for food and to work for people. People who support animal rights believe that this is wrong because animals show feelings, can suffer, and understand what happens to them.

ANIMALS ARE PART OF OUR WORLD AND OUR ECOSYSTEM. LOOKING AFTER OUR PLANET MEANS LOOKING AFTER ANIMALS, TOO.

Positive Changes

Over time, more and more rules have been made to protect animals. In some places, people are not allowed to do tests on animals or use parts of them to make clothes. There are also rules that stop people from catching and killing animals in cruel ways.

One way that people support animal rights is by choosing not to eat meat. People who don't eat meat are called vegetarians. Vegans are people who don't eat or drink anything from animals at all, including milk and eggs.

Small Changes, Big Impacts

Changing the world starts at home. Many things that we use every day are bad for the environment. By making small changes to the way we live, we can have a positive impact.

Glass, plastic, metal, and paper can all be recycled.

Garbage

To keep garbage from going into landfill sites or being burned, we can recycle. Check that the trash in your home is sorted properly.

Energy

Leaving devices on when you are not using them wastes a lot of energy. Save energy by turning lights and other devices off when you leave.

Food Waste

About one-third of the food in the world is wasted. Much of it goes into landfill sites. Planning meals before you shop is a good way to only buy as much food as you need.

Some people use leftover food waste to make compost. Compost is broken-down plants and food that helps plants grow.

Meat

Keeping animals for food has a huge effect on the land and the air. Animals create a lot of waste, and trees are often chopped down to make farms. If you eat a lot of meat, try eating meals with less meat for a while.

CAN YOU THINK OF ANY SMALL CHANGES YOU COULD MAKE AT HOME THAT WOULD HELP THE PLANET?

Making a Change in your Community

Think about the places near you and what positive impacts you could make. Here are some ideas:

Cars

Cars can be a big source of pollution. Walking or biking when we can is a better choice than driving.

Wildlife

There might be some natural spaces near you that are home to different kinds of wildlife. Make sure to look after them by staying on the paths and not treading on them. This is not just your home – it's theirs, too!

NATURAL SPACES ARE PLACES THAT PEOPLE HAVE NOT IMPACTED MUCH, SUCH AS FIELDS, PONDS, AND WOODS.

Trash Can

Sometimes, people leave trash in places they are not supposed to. This is called littering. Littering makes an area look and smell bad. It can even be dangerous to wildlife. Use trash cans when you have garbage to throw away.

Thrift Stores

Huge amounts of clothes get thrown away every day and sent to landfill sites. Make sure to look after your clothes so that they last a long time. When you grow out of them, you can donate them for someone else to use.

VISIT A THRIFT STORE THE NEXT TIME YOU NEED CLOTHES INSTEAD OF BUYING NEW ITEMS.

For the Future

Every small action that we take is important for both now and the future. Many of the problems that the planet faces now are because people before us were not environmentally minded. They were not educated about what their impact on the future would be.

Being environmentally minded now will help the people who come after us.

Sustainability

When we live in a way that protects the future of our planet, that is called being sustainable. Sustainable living includes using resources that will not run out and reusing things we already have.

Pollution and waste is not sustainable. Filling the planet with garbage hurts ecosystems and negatively impacts the future. Many plastics are harmful to wildlife years after they have been thrown away. Before we throw something away, we should see if there is another use for it.

Sustainable Energy

Energy that comes from sunlight is more sustainable than many other options. We can get energy from sunlight by using solar panels. Solar panels do not fill the air with pollution and can be used again and again.

THE WIND AND RIVERS CAN ALSO BE GOOD SOURCES OF SUSTAINABLE ENERGY.

Jobs in Environmentalism

There are many jobs for people who want to look after the planet. To do environmental jobs, people spend a lot of time learning about the science of our planet and everything in it.

For many environmental jobs, people need an education that helps them research. People can start their education at school and continue at a university. They can also work alongside and learn from other environmentalists.

Marine Rescuer

Marine rescuers help protect and care for ocean animals. They learn how to help many different types of animals and their ecosystems. They also have to know the rules about the environment and wildlife in their area.

Marine rescuers often work on beaches to help animals that have become stuck on land get back into the ocean. They also help sick or hurt animals. Sometimes, they help animals that are trapped by garbage in the ocean.

This marine rescuer is helping a dolphin that is stuck on the beach. A wet towel keeps it from drying out.

CONSERVATIONIST

Conservationists work to protect different areas in the environment. They keep track of how many plants and animals are in an area. They have to know what each of them are. Conservationists come up with plans to keep the living things in an area safe and protected.

A big part of a conservationist's job is to teach people about their impact on the environment. If an area is not being properly looked after by the people who live there, a conservationist can come to show them what they can change.

Agronomist

Agronomists are experts on keeping soil healthy and sustainable. They do tests on the land that farmers use to grow crops. Crops are plants that are used for food. Agronomists help farmers change their impact to be more environmentally friendly.

WORDS STARTING WITH "AGRO" USUALLY HAVE TO DO WITH SOIL, FIELDS, OR FARMING.

Environmental Engineer

A lot of the damage to our planet happens because of the way we make buildings. Environmental engineers are people who find ways for these buildings to be as safe for the environment as possible.

This environmental engineer tests how clean the water is in an area.

Tell the World!

Work Together

It is much easier to make changes when we work together. Even a small group of people can make a big difference. The best way to get people to work together to keep the planet clean is by sharing what you know about the environment.

Share What You Love

You can share what you have learned at school, at home, or with your friends. Think about what you love about the planet and tell them all about it.

Your friends might not know about the impact they have on the environment. Some might think that changing the planet is too hard. You can show people that looking after the planet and making positive changes can be fun!

Be an Example

Try to show people some of the small things they can do that make a big impact. Bring your family and friends with you on a walk or a bike ride instead of taking a car. Try new meals that use less meat. You can be an example to people every day by how you live.

Make a Difference

Day by day, we are changing the planet. Everything we do makes an impact, so it is important to make a choice about what kind of impact we want to have. What will you do to have a positive impact on the planet?

Be Inspired

We all make a difference on this planet. Let's make a positive impact!

"WHAT YOU DO MAKES A DIFFERENCE, AND YOU HAVE TO DECIDE WHAT KIND OF DIFFERENCE YOU WANT TO MAKE."

– JANE GOODALL

Glossary

beliefs	strong opinions or thoughts about something
cruel	done without care for any pain caused
donate	to give things or money away to be used by other people
educated	having knowledge about something, often from a school or university
energy	a type of power, such as light or heat, that can be used to do something
environment	the natural world
environmentalists	people who work towards helping the natural world around them
landfill sites	areas of land where waste is buried
nonfiction	a type of book that talks about facts in the real world
observations	things you have noticed around you
pollution	harmful and poisonous things being added to an environment
raise awareness	to bring a lot of attention to something to help cause change
resources	useful materials that come from nature
wildlife	animals and plants

Index

Image Credits

All images are courtesy of Shutterstock.com, unless otherwise specified. With thanks to Getty Images, Thinkstock Photo and iStockphoto. Front Cover – Somchai Som, Dmytro Zinkevych, ixpert, domnitsky, Pixel-Shot, POP-THAILAND, NazArt. 4&5 – hedgehog94, Tapui, Tetiana Savaryn, Tatevosian Yana. 6&7 – Modvector, elenabsl, LightField Studios, vchal, Erni, Rawpixel.com. 8&9 – OV11, wavebreakmedia, Prostock-studio, marikun, Studio Romantic, ARIMAG. 10&11 – Chat Karen Studio, EgudinKa, Belozersky, wavebreakmedia, Tyler Olson, Andrew Angelov, Photodiem, Rido. 12&13 – StockImageFactory.com, Denis Kuvaev, Motortion Films, Krakenimages.com. 14&15 – vladwel, Hafid Firman, Mar1kOFF, Rawpixel.com, Halfpoint, DisobeyArt, RapunzielStock, Maria Symchych. 16&17 – awang_79, GoodStudio, Simon Eeman, Rawpixel.com, TetiBond, Prostock-studio, JLco Julia Amaral, Yulia Kozlova. 18&19 – N.Savranska, Jayakri, Artazum, Jerome.Romme, Kletr, SGr. 20&21 – Hayran1, Anastasiia Cherviak, Walnut Bird. 22&23 – Supriya07, DidGason, Monkey Business Images, Toey Toey, RenataP. 24&25 – Shanvood, Pogorelova Olga, Sia Footage, Tunatura, N center, Studio Romantic. 26&27 – topvector, BalanceFormCreative, Sunti, Budimir Jevtic, kittirat roekburi. 28&29 – Betty Ray, YAKOBCHUK VIACHESLAV, Robert Kneschke, Monkey Business Images, Dmytro Zinkevych, wavebreakmedia. 30 – Halfpoint, Jeekc, CC BY-SA 3.0 <http://creativecommons.org/licenses/by-sa/3.0/>, via Wikimedia Commons.